Dikembe Mutombo

by Mark Stewart

ACKNOWLEDGMENTS

The editors wish to thank Dikembe Mutombo for his cooperation in preparing this book.
Thanks also to Integrated Sports International for their assistance.

PHOTO CREDITS

All photos courtesy AP/Wide World Photos, Inc. except the following:

Vince Manniello/Sports Chrome – Cover, 6
Mitchell Layton/Georgetown University – 13, 24 top left
CARE – 43
Sports Media, Inc. – 5 bottom right, 46 bottom right
Mark Stewart – 48

STAFF

Project Coordinator: John Sammis, Cronopio Publishing
Series Design Concept: The Sloan Group
Design and Electronic Page Makeup: Jaffe Enterprises, and
        Digital Communications Services, Inc.

LIBRARY OF CONGRESS CATALOGING-IN-PUBLICATION DATA

Stewart, Mark.
    Dikembe Mutombo / by Mark Stewart.
        p. cm. – (Grolier all-pro biographies)
    Includes index.
    Summary: A biography of the native Zairian who never picked up a basketball until he was sixteen
years of age but learned the game quickly and became an All-Star.
    ISBN 0-516-20168-9 (lib. binding) – ISBN 0-516-26016-2 (pbk.)
    1. Mutombo, Dikembe–Juvenile literature. 2. Basketball players–United States–Biography–
Juvenile literature. 3. Denver Nuggets (Basketball team)–Juvenile literature. [1. Mutombo, Dikembe.
2. Basketball players. 3. Denver Nuggets (basketball team) 4. Blacks–Zaire–Biography.] I. Title.
II. Series.
GV884.M886S84 1996
796.323'092–dc20
[B]   96-14050
                                                                               CIP
                                                                               AC

Grolier **ALL-PRO** Biographies™

Dikembe

Mutombo

by
Mark Stewart

CHILDREN'S PRESS®
A Division of Grolier Publishing
New York • London • Hong Kong • Sydney
Danbury, Connecticut

Contents

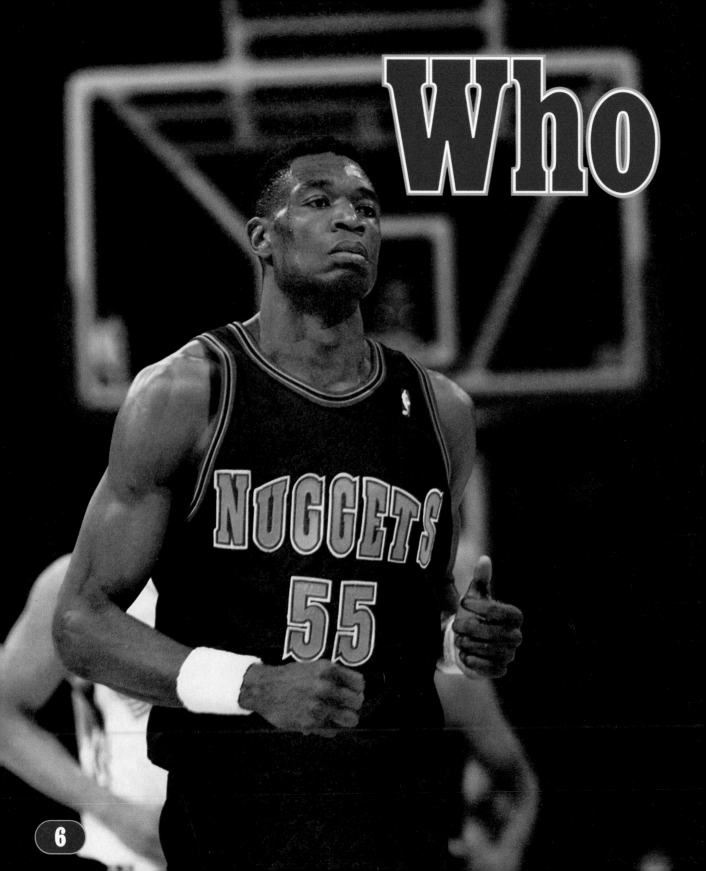

Who

Am I?

In America, many children dream of becoming a basketball star. In my country, there were no basketball stars, so when I was young, I dreamed of becoming a doctor. At first, basketball was just a way to get a good education. But as I worked hard and learned the game, it became my career. My name is Dikembe Mutombo, and this is my story . . . "

"When I was young, I dreamed of becoming a doctor."

Growing Up

Modern buildings in Dikembe's home city, Kinshasa, Zaire

How many NBA All-Stars can say they never dribbled a basketball before the age of 16? Dikembe Mutombo is probably the only one. That is because he never wanted to be a professional athlete—Dikembe wanted to become a doctor. For most of his young life, he concentrated on his studies and hardly gave sports a second thought. That was fine with his father, who was an important official in the school system of Kinshasa, the capital city of the African country called Zaire.

Education was far more important than athletics in Dikembe's home, but that did not mean that Dikembe did not love sports. When he was eight years old, he saw Muhammad Ali defeat George Foreman for the heavyweight championship. The bout was held in the stadium across the street from his house. His mother owned a concession stand at the stadium, so he and his brothers got to watch the fight for free!

Dikembe was a very serious student who loved to learn. From an early age, he realized how fun and important reading is. "Reading

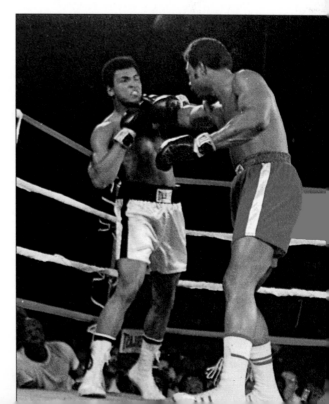

The Muhammad Ali–George Foreman fight was held across the street from Dikembe's home.

is the most important thing you will ever learn," says Dikembe. "You must be able to read simply to function. You may not realize it now, but you will have to read something nearly every minute of your life."

Dikembe found science and math fascinating, even though he had trouble memorizing his multiplication tables and working with fractions. He solved this problem by reciting them before he went to sleep. By the time Dikembe reached high school, he had decided that he wanted to become a doctor.

At the age of 16, Dikembe transferred to the Boboto Institute, which offered very challenging math and science courses. His favorite teacher at the school, however, taught civics. From this teacher, Dikembe learned to take responsibility for his actions, and to accept blame and praise equally. These were lessons that would serve him well throughout his life.

Dikembe grew up with his five brothers and two sisters in a large house in downtown Kinshasa. Everyone in the family was very tall, but Dikembe was the tallest. Most of the children in Kinshasa played soccer, but Dikembe was too big and clumsy to keep up with the smaller, quicker players. When he did play soccer, he played goalie, where he could use his long arms to block shots.

Dikembe's brother, Ilo, told him that he should try basketball. Ilo was one of the best basketball players in the city. He tried to convince Dikembe that he could block shots in basketball, just like in soccer. His father, Mukambe, also encouraged Dikembe to give the sport a try, especially when Ilo informed him that American universities would gladly give a player of Dikembe's size a scholarship if he showed some talent for the game.

The two brothers went to a nearby court, and Ilo began teaching Dikembe the basics of basketball. The first thing they tried was a simple jumping drill. Dikembe started well enough, but then fell flat on his face! No, he thought, this game was not for him.

Slowly but surely, Dikembe came to enjoy basketball. At first, he tagged along with Ilo when he went to practice. Then he started watching highlight tapes of American basketball games. Soon, Dikembe was playing side-by-side with his brother on the Zairian national basketball team. He recalls, "I traveled to various countries with my national team as a teenager for two years. I was the youngest on the team, but I was just traveling with them, learning how to play basketball."

Just as Ilo had predicted, college recruiters from the United States began attending their games.

As he became more involved in basketball and began traveling with the national team, Dikembe had to work even harder to keep up with his studies. Then came the chance to go to the United States. In 1987, Dikembe was offered a full scholarship to Georgetown University, near Washington, D.C. It was the perfect place for him—it had a strong basketball program, a patient coach, and one of the best medical schools in the world. Dikembe hoped to continue balancing basketball and schoolwork at Georgetown. His plan was to graduate from college, and then choose between a career in medicine or basketball.

Dikembe's desire to complete a college education came from his family. "Almost everybody in my family has finished college," he says proudly. "My best friend was my younger brother. He made me realize that I am a role model and I must take that responsibility seriously."

Dikembe was always taller than his classmates. He could dunk a basketball long before he arrived at Georgetown University.

College

Dikembe Mutombo was 21 years old when he enrolled at Georgetown University. Many of the students in his class were just 17 and 18, but they had one advantage Dikembe did not have: they spoke English. So in addition to his regular courses, he studied English seven hours a day. Dikembe would not have had the time to do this had he been playing basketball. But because he did not read English well enough to pass the college-entrance test, he was not allowed to play for the Georgetown Hoyas during his freshman year. Ironically, he could have passed easily had he been allowed to take the test in Spanish, which he already spoke fluently!

In order to stay in shape, Dikembe played intramural basketball against other Georgetown students. The competition was good, but not nearly as tough as what he would face in his sophomore season. Still, Dikembe improved dramatically. By the end of the season, he was regularly scoring 30 points and pulling down 15 rebounds per game. That summer, he signed

Years

up for a local league in which many pro and college stars competed. Before the first game, some players heard a rumor that Dikembe was less than six feet tall. You can imagine their surprise when they first saw the 7' 2" center!

When Dikembe began playing for the Georgetown Hoyas in his sophomore year, it was both a relief and a disappointment. He was happy to finally have the chance to play, but he soon realized that the practice and travel schedule of the Hoyas would not permit him to continue his study of medicine.

Dikembe played about 10 minutes a game that year, and he worked hard with coach John Thompson to improve. He practiced for several hours each week against the team's freshman center, Alonzo Mourning, who helped him tremendously. Alonzo was already an excellent player, and he taught Dikembe some of the secrets of the position.

Alonzo Mourning helped Dikembe learn the fine points of the game.

Off the court, Dikembe decided that if he could not be a doctor, he would represent Zaire in the foreign service. He already spoke English, French, Spanish, Portuguese, and five African languages. Dikembe began taking courses that would lead to a degree in diplomacy. During the summer, he took jobs that would help him in this new career. Prior to his junior year, Dikembe worked as an intern on Capitol Hill; a summer later, he worked for the World Bank, helping with translations.

Dikembe's game improved dramatically during his junior year. He became an expert shot-blocker, and learned how to box out quicker opponents to get important rebounds. He even developed a hook shot, which enabled him to average more than 10 points a game. Because Dikembe could only play the center position, Alonzo Mourning had to move to

By his senior year, Dikembe had become a dominant rebounder and shot-blocker.

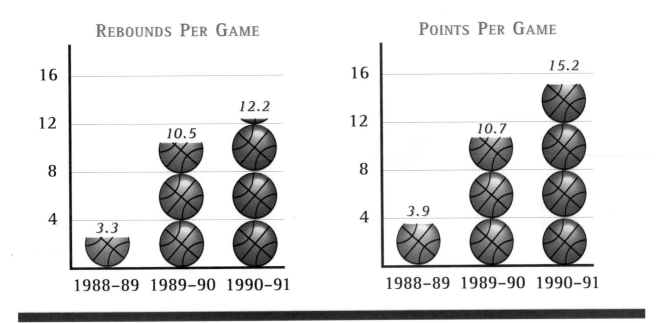

REBOUNDS PER GAME

POINTS PER GAME

power forward whenever both were in the game. At first, this caused some confusion. But by the end of the season, they were playing well together and the team finished with an impressive 24–7 record. As a senior, Dikembe improved his scoring to 15.2 points per game, and he became a dominant rebounder, averaging better than 12 per contest. He also gained a new understanding of basketball, finally getting to the point where he could feel the flow of the game. Dikembe's diplomatic career would have to wait—he was certain to be selected in the first round of the 1991 NBA draft.

The Story

Dikembe Mutombo was the fourth player selected in the 1991 NBA draft. His new team would be the Denver Nuggets, a franchise that had struggled in recent years. In 1990–91, the Nuggets had won just 20 games. Under coach Paul Westhead, the team used a "run-and-gun" offense that produced 111.9 points a game. But the Nuggets spent so much time shooting, they had trouble playing defense at the other end. In 1990–91, the team had given up an average of 130.8 points a night! Coach Westhead was not sure how well Dikembe would score in the NBA, but he was sure that his new center would provide the team with the defensive "stopper" it so desperately needed.

NBA commissioner David Stern congratulates Dikembe, who was picked fourth in the 1991 NBA draft.

Dikembe put his hook shot to good use during his rookie year with the Nuggets.

Continues

o the great delight of Denver fans and teammates, Dikembe played better than anyone could have imagined. As a rookie, he was the top rebounder among NBA centers, and his 16.6 points per game was second on the Nuggets to forward Reggie Williams (who had also played for Georgetown). The biggest contribution Dikembe made was on defense. Teams could no longer drive down the middle and expect to get an easy basket or a cheap foul—Dikembe made sure of that. When the season was over, the Nuggets had given up 23 points per game less than they had the year before.

Dikembe's rebounding in 1992–93 helped Denver post 12 more wins than they had in 1991–92.

Dikembe was disappointed when he did not win the Rookie of the Year Award, but he had achieved all of the other goals he had set for his first NBA season. As he started his second year, his goal was to make the playoffs. The team was young and lacked confidence, but he felt he could step up and provide the leadership it needed. The Nuggets improved by 12 wins in 1992–93 but fell just short of the playoffs. In 1993–94, they made it, with a respectable 42–40 record.

In the first round of the 1994 playoffs, the Nuggets had to play the Seattle Supersonics, a team everyone said would win the NBA championship. That did not frighten Dikembe. He knew his job was to play fierce defense against Seattle's talented front line of Shawn Kemp, Sam Perkins, Michael Cage, and Detlef Schrempf. Yet despite Dikembe's best efforts, the Supersonics overwhelmed the inexperienced Nuggets and easily won the first two games of the series. One more loss and Denver would be out of the playoffs.

ikembe decided he would not let that happen. In Game Three, he took his game to a new level, blocking shot after shot and pulling down every rebound in sight. Denver surprised the Sonics with a 17-point blowout. Dikembe played even better in the next game, as the Nuggets won a tense overtime battle to tie the series at 2–2. In the fifth and deciding contest, Dikembe again dominated from start to finish, blocking eight Seattle shots, including two in a wild overtime period. When the final buzzer sounded, Denver was the winner . . . and Dikembe was a basketball legend. In the five-game series, he led all players with 61 rebounds and

In 1995, Dikembe was the top shot-blocker in the NBA.

set an all-time playoff record with 31 blocks.

"After losing two games, I told the media that I'd had a dream we had won the series. They just said, 'No way, Mutombo, you can't match up with Seattle.' But I had seen the game in my sleep and we had won, and then I saw us celebrating, so I knew we had won the series."

In the next series, the Nuggets lost the first three games to the Utah

After winning Defensive Player of the Year in 1994–95, Dikembe continued his rebounding domination in 1995–96.

Jazz despite Dikembe's tremendous effort. But then Denver came roaring back to tie the series. Dikembe was heartbroken when he and his teammates lost the seventh and deciding game of the series. Still, he set another record for blocked shots, with a total of 38.

Dikembe has continued to dominate on defense. He was the NBA's top shot-blocker in 1993–94, and again in 1994–95, when he also led the league with 1,029 rebounds and was named Defensive Player of the Year. Dikembe can be a scary fellow when you have to go head-to-head with him. But what is even scarier is that he is still learning the game . . . and getting better each year!

Timeline

1987: Enrolls at Georgetown University

1990: Named Big East Co-Defensive Player of the Year with teammate Alonzo Mourning

1991: Joins the NBA Denver Nuggets

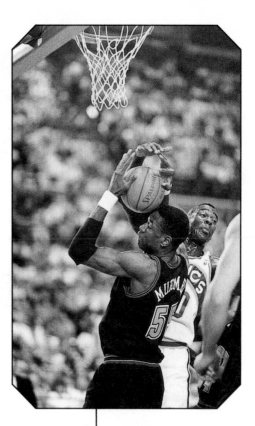

1995: Named NBA Defensive Player of the Year

1992: Makes the All-Star team in his rookie year

1994: Leads the NBA in blocked shots

Game

What Dikembe does best does not show up in his stats. He is as good as anyone in the league at intimidating opponents who drive the lane.

Dikembe's best shot is his jump-hook. First developed in college, it is now a potent offensive weapon.

Action!

Georgetown coach John Thompson had a great influence on Dikembe.

Dikembe does not fool around when he gets the ball near the basket— he will jam over anyone in the league.

Dikembe loves to prove his critics wrong. "Why did people say I would not score in the NBA? I don't know. I can grab offensive rebounds and put them back in, if nothing else."

Dikembe is one of four top centers to emerge from Georgetown in recent years. Patrick Ewing (center), Alonzo Mourning, and Othella Harrington are the others.

Dikembe simply refuses to allow easy layups. If someone tries to go to the hoop against the Nuggets—even Shaquille O'Neal (left)—he can expect to see number 55 come flying toward him.

When I first came into the league, I didn't get respect. I think I showed the world what I was capable of."

Dikembe puts back a rebound against Cleveland's Chris Mills.

I want to know I can approach my coach sometimes, and that he can tell me, 'Big fella, look what you're doing, it's no good.'"

Dikembe refuses to give ground, even to superstar Hakeem Olajuwon.

Dealing

ikembe Mutombo is not happy with the way Zaire and other African countries are portrayed in magazines and on television in the United States. The vast majority of Africans do not live in mud huts, but in cities and towns similar to most American communities. But how can one man change the ideas of millions? One person at a time. In the summer of 1994, Dikembe took his friends Patrick Ewing and Alonzo Mourning on an eye-opening trip to Africa.

"I think they realized then that I didn't come from the jungle. I come from a really modern culture where I was aware of everything that was happening when I was growing up."

Dikembe teaches a youngster the finer points of basketball during a 1993 tour of Africa.

With It

How Does

He Do It?

Dikembe Mutombo is sometimes criticized for playing off his man so he has a better chance of blocking shots, but this is a risk that he feels is worth taking. In his mind, a blocked shot does a lot more than just keep the other side from scoring.

"It doesn't just make me feel good, but my teammates, too. It gets the team excited and changes the tempo of the game. It makes me feel like I'm doing what I was brought into this organization to do."

After playing off his man, Dikembe comes across the baseline to block Gheorghe Muresan's shot. Dikembe believes that a blocked shot can fire up a team more than any other play.

The Grind

Dikembe Mutombo is in such great physical condition that he can play hard all game without getting tired. To do that takes rest and relaxation between games—something that is not always easy for Dikembe to do. When he wants to unwind at a movie or go shopping, the seven-footer attracts fans like a magnet. What starts as an afternoon of leisure can quickly turn into a stressful situation.

"Fans don't understand that sometimes you need just five or ten minutes of privacy."

Kids crowd into a gym to hear Dikembe speak.

36

The seven-foot-tall Dikembe attracts attention wherever he goes.

Say What?

Here's what basketball people say about Dikembe Mutombo:

"The best thing about coaching this basketball team is that the best player, Dikembe, is the player who works the hardest in practice. That's a marvelous influence on the rest of the team."

—Dan Issel,
*   former Denver Nuggets coach*

"Mutombo is huge. When he plays behind you, it's hard to even see the basket!"

—Larry Brown, Indiana Pacers coach

"He hustles all the time, and he has what you can't teach, and that's heart."

—*John Thompson,*
  Georgetown University coach

"He's quick to the ball and really loves to get it."

—*Bob Babcock, Denver Nuggets scout*

"There aren't many big men around who can move like he can."

—*Jerry West, NBA Hall of Famer*

"There's nobody else in our league who has his intimidating presence in the hole. He's one of a kind."

—*Don Nelson,*
  longtime NBA coach

Dikembe was the only rookie selected to play in the 1992 NBA All-Star Game.

Dikembe led the NBA with 336 blocked shots during the 1993–94 season. He also made 56.9 percent of his shots, the second-best mark in the league.

Highlights

Dikembe played brilliantly in the 1993–94 playoffs. His 31 blocks against the Seattle Supersonics set an NBA record for a five-game series, and his 38 blocks against the Utah Jazz established a new mark for a seven-game series.

Dikembe was voted the NBA's 1994–95 Defensive Player of the Year.

Dikembe did it all in the 1995 All-Star Game. In only 20 minutes, he scored 12 points, collected eight rebounds, and swatted away four shots.

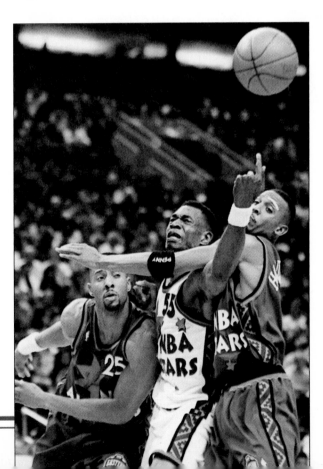

Dikembe fights Alonzo Mourning (right) and Penny Hardaway (left) for a loose ball during the 1995 All-Star Game.

Reaching

ikembe Mutombo's father once told him that he should always try to give something back. He followed his father's advice the moment he arrived in Denver, making himself available to many local charities. Dikembe is the team spokesman for the Denver Nuggets' "Stay-in-School" program, which takes him to classrooms all over the city.

"I work with as many different organizations as I can, including CARE, Children's Hospital, Special Olympics, Boys and Girls Clubs, and the Make a Wish Foundation."

Dikembe and Washington Bullets Hall of Famer Wes Unseld (top photo, right) tour the CARE project in Zambia, Africa. CARE is the world's largest private relief and development organization.

Out

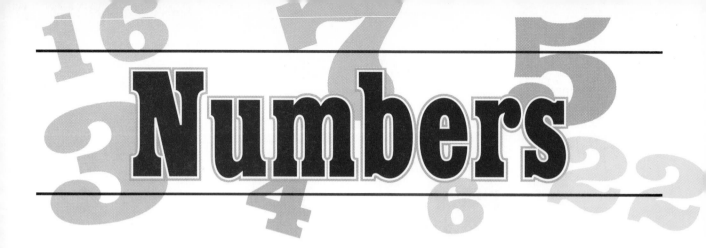

Numbers

Name: Dikembe Mutombo Mpolondo Mukamba Jean Jacque Wamutombo

Born: June 25, 1966   **Uniform Number:** 55

Height: 7' 2"   **College:** Georgetown University

Weight: 250 pounds

Dikembe is definitely built for basketball. From fingertip to fingertip, his arms measure 7' 6" and his body fat has been calculated at just 1.9 percent of his total body weight. He also wears size-20 sneakers!

Year	Team	Games	Rebounds	Rebounds Per Game	Blocks	Blocks Per Game
1991–92	Denver Nuggets	71	870	12.3	210	3.0
1992–93	Denver Nuggets	82	1,070	13.0	287	3.5
1993–94	Denver Nuggets	82	971	11.8	336*	4.1*
1994–95	Denver Nuggets	82	1,029*	12.5	321*	3.9*
1995–96	Denver Nuggets	74	871	11.8	332*	4.5*
Totals		391	4,811	12.3	1,486	3.8

*Led the league

What If...

If I had never been introduced to the game of basketball, I know exactly what I would be doing today. I would be a medical doctor in my native Africa. Had I not made it in the NBA, I would have had an interesting choice. The classes I took in college would have enabled me to pursue a diplomatic career—in fact, after my rookie season, I returned to Georgetown to take graduate courses in diplomacy and political science. So I could have continued along that path, or returned to my medical studies."

Glossary

FRANCHISE a team with a legal license to play in a professional league

GRADUATE COURSES the courses of study one takes after graduating from college in order to achieve higher academic degrees

DIPLOMACY the art of conducting and regulating relationships between countries

FOREIGN SERVICE group of government workers who deal in our country's relationships with other nations

POTENT powerful; effective

RECRUITER one who tries to get people to join their team or organization

SAT TEST a test given to all high-school students in the United States before entering college

SCHOLARSHIP money given to a student to help pay for schooling

INELIGIBLE not possessing the necessary qualifications to join a team or organization; unqualified

INTERN an on-the-job trainee who receives school credit for his work

PATIENT having the ability to put up with trouble or delay without getting angry or upset

POLITICAL SCIENCE the study of governments and how they operate

TRANSLATION expressing words of one language in another language

 Index

About The Author

Mark Stewart grew up in New York City in the 1960s and 1970s—when the Mets, Jets, and Knicks all had championship teams. As a child, Mark read everything about sports he could lay his hands on. Today, he is one of the busiest sportswriters around. Since 1990, he has written close to 500 sports stories for kids, including profiles on more than 200 athletes, past and present. A graduate of Duke University, Mark served as senior editor of *Racquet*, a national tennis magazine, and was managing editor of *Super News*, a sporting goods industry newspaper. He is the author of every Grolier All-Pro Biography.